Foods of Pakistan

Barbara Sheen

KIDHAVEN PRESS
A part of Gale, Cengage Learning

GALE
CENGAGE Learning

Detroit • New York • San Francisco • New Haven, Conn • Waterville, Maine • London

GALE
CENGAGE Learning™

LIBRARY OF CONGRESS CATALOGING-IN-PUBLICATION DATA

Sheen, Barbara.
 Foods of Pakistan / by Barbara Sheen.
   p. cm. -- (A taste of culture)
 Includes bibliographical references and index.
 ISBN 978-0-7377-5883-2 (hardcover)
 1. Cooking, Pakistani--Juvenile literature. 2. Pakistan--Social life and customs--Juvenile literature. 3. Cookbooks--Juvenile literature. 4. Children's cookbooks. I. Title.
 TX724.5.P3S54 2011
 641.595491--dc23

 2011014611

Kidhaven Press
27500 Drake Rd.
Farmington Hills MI 48331

ISBN-13: 978-0-7377-5883-2
ISBN-10: 0-7377-5883-X

Printed in the United States of America
1 2 3 4 5 6 7 15 14 13 12 11

Printed by Bang Printing, Brainerd, MN, 1st Ptg., 07/2011

Contents

An Artful Blend

Pakistan is a country in southern Asia with a long history. It did not become an independent nation until 1947, but the land that is now known as Pakistan has been the home of some of the world's great ancient cultures. Since 3000 B.C. Pakistani cooks have used spices, wheat, legumes, and meat to create delicious and fragrant dishes.

Spices

Throughout history, people have traveled to southern Asia for spices. Their journeys were often long and dangerous. Unlike spice seekers from other areas of the world, Pakistani cooks never had to travel far for spices,

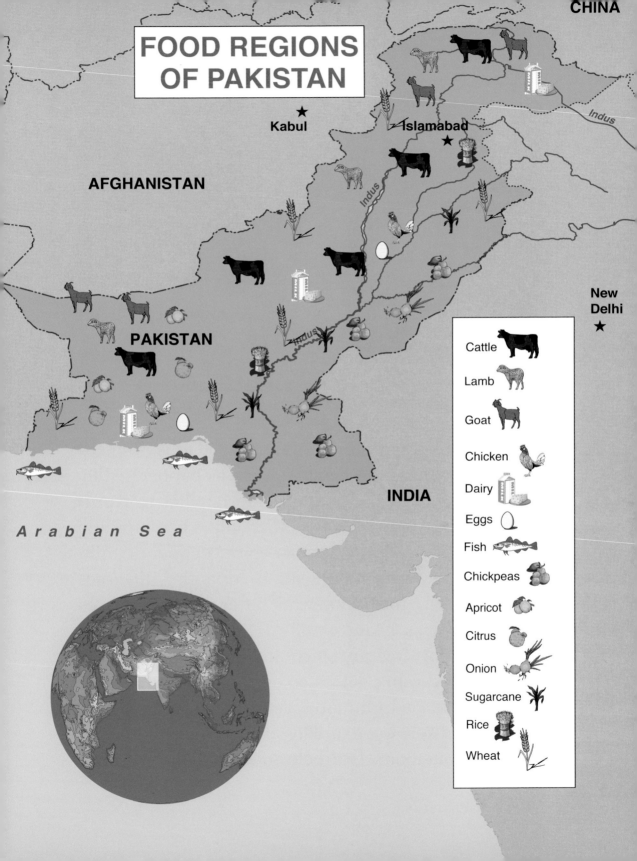

A man sells colorful spices mounded in bowls at a market in Pakistan. A range of flavorful spices, including cayenne pepper, cumin, garlic, and mint, are used in Pakistani cooking.

because Pakistan produces about 45,300 tons of spices per year. Some of these spices, such as pepper, garlic, mustard seeds, and cinnamon, are familiar to North Americans. Less familiar are other spices like turmeric (TER-mer-ick), a bitter orange spice; peppery cumin (COO-men); warm, mildly sweet coriander (KOR-ee-ann-der) seeds; fresh somewhat bitter coriander leaves (also known as cilantro; sill-AHN-troh); and carda-mom, a strong, fragrant spice similar to ginger.

These and other spices color, flavor, and perfume almost every Pakistani food. Pakistani cooking, which ranges from fiery hot to mildly spiced, would not be the same without them. An article on KhanaPakana.com, a

Fast Facts About Pakistan

Pakistan's official name is the Islamic Republic of Pakistan. It borders the Arabian Sea in the south, India in the east, Iran and Afghanistan in the west, and China in the north. It is the sixth most populous country in the world. In area, it is a little smaller than twice the size of California. Its climate is hot and dry in most of the country with summer temperatures reaching 120°F (49°C). The temperature in the northern mountains, however, is extremely cold.

Urdu is Pakistan's national language. Its capital is Islamabad and its largest city is Karachi. Its currency is the rupee. About 49 percent of Pakistanis are literate (can read and write). Of these, 63 percent are male and 36 percent are female. About 24 percent of Pakistanis live below the poverty level.

website dedicated to Pakistani cooking, puts it this way: "Fried red cayenne pepper, cumin and mustard seeds, crushed garlic cloves with freshly cut mint, onion slivers and coriander leaves—these are the aromas of most Pakistani kitchens."[1]

Masala

With so many spices to choose from, Pakistani cooks rarely use just one spice in their cooking. They blend a number of spices together to create a mixture of ground spices known as a **masala** (mah-SAH-lah). The amounts and combinations depend on the cook. The

A mix of spices are ground together using a mortar and pestle to create garam masala, one of several types of masala used to flavor Pakistani dishes.

goal is for the spices to taste good together and improve the flavor of the food. To achieve this requires being familiar with the flavors of the spices. Author Huma Siddiqui explains: "It is critical to be aware of the spices as separate ingredients and what they taste like."[2]

Pakistani cooks make different types of masalas. Garam masala (GAH-rahm mah-SAH-lah), which means hot spices, is very popular. It typically contains five spices. Cardamom, cloves, cumin, coriander seeds, and black pepper make up a popular combination. Chaat masala (chaht mah-SAH-lah) is another popular blend. It is a tart and zesty mix with a fruity aroma. It is likely to contain cumin, ginger, coriander, and amchur (AHM-choor), which is a powder made from dried green mangos.

To make masala, cooks grind different spices together into a powder. This may be done the old-fashioned way, with the chef crushing the spices using a small club-like tool called a **pestle** in a stone dish called a **mortar**. Or, a modern food processor may be used.

Besides grinding spices, Pakistani cooks fry whole spices in sizzling hot oil. The oil, which is known as **tarka**, is poured over foods. It adds a spicy flavor and a delicious scent.

The Birth of Modern Pakistan

It took thousands of years for the modern nation of Pakistan to be created. Five thousand years ago the land that is now Pakistan was part of the Indus Valley Civilization. It was an advanced civilization with great cities, and advanced sanitation, water, and measuring systems.

Pakistan was also part of Greek, Persian, Arab, Ottoman (Turkish), and Indian kingdoms. It was part of the powerful Moghul Empire, which covered Pakistan, India, and Afghanistan, from the 16th century until 1858. The Moghuls were from central Asia and are believed to be related to the 13th-century Mongolian ruler Genghis Khan.

After the Moghuls, the British ruled Pakistan and India as one nation. In 1947 the British divided the area into two independent nations: One was India, whose people are mostly Hindus. The other country was Pakistan, whose people are mostly Muslims. At that point, the modern nation of Pakistan was born.

Meat

Beef and lamb dishes are another popular part of Pakistani cooking. Spices are added to meat to boost the flavor, texture, and aroma. Pakistanis eat meat every chance they get. Their love of meat is one of the biggest differences between their cooking and that of neighboring India, even though the two were once one nation. Pakistanis eat about three times as much meat as do Indians. Pork, however, is rarely eaten. Most Pakistanis are Muslims, who follow the religion of **Islam**. Islamic laws forbid Muslims from eating pork.

Pakistanis grill meat, roast it, top it with spicy sauces and sizzling oil, or slowly stew it. Nihari (nee-HAH-

Beef nihari is a type of stew commonly eaten for breakfast in Pakistan.

ree), a spicy beef stew that is slowly cooked overnight, is a popular breakfast dish. Cooking meat in spices serves many purposes. Spices add flavor to the meat, help keep it from spoiling, and make it tender. Slow cooking also makes meat tender. Not surprisingly, the meat in nihari is buttery soft.

Nutritious Legumes

Legumes, such as beans, lentils, and peas, also play a key role in the Pakistani people's diet. In the 1970s a civil war in Pakistan caused a meat shortage. In order to cope, the government made everyone eat two meatless meals each week. Legumes, which are loaded with protein and other nutrients, replaced the meat. When the war ended, Pakistanis continued eating lots of lentils, which they now often cook with meat.

Pakistani cooks use many different types of legumes. Split peas, yellow and pink lentils, and garbanzo beans (also known as chickpeas) are top choices. One of the most popular ways of preparing legumes is in **dal** (dahl). Dal is a creamy stew-like dish. To make it, cooks soak legumes in water overnight to soften them. Then they cook the legumes over low heat for hours. When the legumes are meltingly soft, they are topped with tarka. The tarka adds flavor to the otherwise bland legumes.

Each cook makes dal differently, so there are hundreds of variations. According to one Pakistani legend, the many varieties of dal once helped an imprisoned king. In an effort to make the king's time in prison as

Chana Dal

Chana dal is dal made with garbanzo beans. For a heartier dish, potatoes or peas can be added to the mixture.

Ingredients
1 can (15 ounces) garbanzo beans, drained
4 tablespoons olive oil
⅓ onion, chopped
4 garlic cloves, chopped
1 medium tomato, chopped
½ teaspoon chili powder
½ teaspoon coriander
¼ teaspoon cumin
water

Instructions
1. Put the beans in a pot. Add enough water to cover the beans.
2. Cook uncovered on low heat until most of the liquid has been absorbed.
3. Heat the remaining two tablespoons of oil in a frying pan over medium heat. Add the onion, tomato, garlic, and spices. Cook until the onions are translucent, or nearly clear.
4. Put the beans in bowls. Pour the oil mixture on top of the beans. Stir before eating.

Serves 4.

The ingredients of chana dal include (clockwise, from left) onion, spices, tomato, and garbanzo beans.

Tarka dal is a stew-like dish made with several types of legumes and topped with flavored oil.

unpleasant as possible, his captors decided to feed him only one food. So, the king asked for dal. With all the varieties, the king never had to eat the same meal twice!

Any combination of legumes and spices can be used to make dal. The dish can be made with one legume or many types of legumes. Bits of meat and/or vegetables can be added, too. Orange lentils mixed with fried onions and tomatoes and topped with turmeric and ginger tarka is one choice. Yellow lentils cooked with spinach and topped with cumin and garlic tarka is another.

All varieties are usually served over rice, sprinkled

with fresh coriander leaves, a squeeze of lemon juice, and a spoonful of raita (RYE-tah), a sauce made with yogurt and spices. The result is a delicious dish that is filling enough to be a complete meal, but light enough for smaller appetites. Pakistani food blogger Shayma calls it "soft, warm, velvety food."[3]

Wheat

Wheat, too, is important to Pakistanis. Fritters, puddings, pastries, and, most importantly, bread, are made with wheat. Hot, fresh bread is a part of almost every meal in Pakistan. And, since Pakistanis do not usually use utensils, bread serves as a tool for sopping up sauces and scooping up food.

Pakistanis make many different types of bread. **Roti** (RO-tee) is probably the most popular. Roti is round flat bread. It is cooked on a flat iron griddle, known as a **tawa** or on the inner

A Pakistani man holds a fresh loaf of naan that was baked in of tandoor, a beehive-shaped clay oven heated with wood and charcoal.

Roti

Roti is not difficult to make. For the best roti, the pan or griddle should be very hot. Roti can be made with whole-wheat flour or all-purpose flour, or a combination. Spices can be added to the dough. Roti hardens quickly. Eat it while it is still hot.

Ingredients
½ cup whole-wheat flour
½ cup all-purpose flour
1 tablespoon olive oil
¼ cup, plus 2 tablespoons water
pinch of salt

Instructions
1. Mix together all the ingredients. Knead the dough for 5 to 10 minutes and until it is smooth and elastic.
2. Cover the dough with a clean dishtowel and let it stand at room temperature for 30 to 45 minutes.
3. Knead the dough. Divide the dough into four balls. On a lightly floured surface, roll out each ball, making it as thin as possible.
4. Heat a nonstick griddle or pan until it is very hot. Put in the roti. Cook each side for 30 seconds or until brown spots form on the bottom. Flip the roti a third time, to get it to rise.

Makes 4 rotis.

walls of a **tandoor**, a beehive-shaped clay oven that is heated with wood or charcoal and can reach temperatures as high as 850°F (450°C). The high heat allows the bread to bake quickly. Traditionally, the woman of the house makes fresh roti with every meal. The best roti is paper-thin, crisp on the outside and soft within. Imaan, who lives in Pakistan, describes how roti is made: "Auntie … rolled pats of dough into little balls and then expertly pinched them to form flat rounds. These were then flipped quickly from one hand to the other in a clapping motion to make them thinner and then speedily slapped on the walls of the tandoor to bake. All done completely by hand with nary a rolling pin."[4]

Naan (nahn) is also often baked on the walls of a tandoor. It is similar to roti but contains yeast. Other popular breads are fried. Puri (POOH-ree) is pancake-like bread that puffs up like a blowfish when it is fried. Pastry-like paratha (pah-RAH-tah) is often stuffed with spicy potatoes or eggs and served for breakfast. They are crispy, flaky, and zesty all at the same time. One Pakistani blogger named Halai says, "We have some of the best forms of bread in the world. . . . Pakistani food in its various forms is an art."[5]

Indeed, the way Pakistani cooks blend together spices, meat, legumes, and wheat takes skill and talent. For thousands of years, Pakistani cooks have depended on these staple ingredients to create delicious meals.

Chapter 2

A Cultural Exchange

Different groups of people have helped shape Pakistani history, culture, and cooking styles. Since ancient times, many people have passed through, invaded, settled in, or ruled over what is now Pakistan. These include the Greeks, Persians, Arabs, **Moghuls**, Indians, and the British. People from neighboring Afghanistan and China have also made an impact. And, because India and Pakistan were once one nation, there is much that the two nations share. The Pakistani people's favorite dishes reflect this cultural exchange.

Curry

Curry, which is also known as salaan in Pakistan, is probably the most famous of all Pakistani dishes. Curry is not one dish, but describes any dish in which meat, chicken, fish, or vegetables are cooked in a spicy sauce. In fact, the word curry means sauce in **Urdu**, Pakistan's national language.

Curry-making developed in India and Pakistan's eastern provinces as a way to keep meat and fish from spoiling in the region's hot climate. Author Jennifer Brennan explains:

A curry dish made with lamb is served over rice. Pakistani cooks make several kinds of curry dishes.

Halal and Haram Foods

Most Pakistanis are Muslims who follow the Islamic religion. The *Koran* is Islam's holy book. It sets down rules about what foods Muslims can and cannot eat. Foods that are allowed are said to be *halal*, or lawful. Those that are forbidden are said to be *haram*. Haram foods include pork and any pork products such as gelatin; animal's blood; any meat from animals who are meat eaters, such as lions, bears, dogs, rats, hyenas, and monkeys; birds of prey; and land animals without external ears, including snakes and insects. Also forbidden is the meat of animals killed by an accident, meat of animals killed by other animals, and the meat of animals who were strangled to death. Alcoholic beverages are also haram.

To be halal, animals must be killed in a humane way that causes the animal as little pain as possible. This involves quickly cutting the major arteries in the animal's throat, which causes all the blood to drain out of its body.

Before the advent of refrigeration it was discovered that if meats . . . were cooked with generous amounts of certain spices it would delay their deterioration. . . . If not cooked immediately, fresh meat, bought in the market in the cool of the early morning, will start to spoil before the hot, tropical sun has crossed the noon sky. . . . So, out of necessity, the process of curry-making evolved.[6]

To make curry, Pakistani cooks fry a mixture of spices with onions. Then they add water and the main ingredients, such as beef or lamb. The mixture is cooked slowly until all the flavors combine. Pakistanis make two types of curry—wet and dry. Wet curry has a thin sauce. The sauce in dry curry is cooked until it almost evaporates. What is left thickens and covers the meat with a colorful spicy coating. Wet curry is served over rice, which absorbs the sauce, while dry curry is scooped up with breads such as roti or naan.

Curry can contain a wide range of ingredients and spices. Pakistani cooks rarely follow a recipe when making curry. In fact, it is unlikely that any two dishes will taste exactly alike. "Ask a Pakistani cook how much spice to use in curry and her answer will be, 'Bus, andaza se,' or 'Well, just use your instinct,'"[7] explains Pakistani journalist Huma Qureshi.

Many Dishes

There are lots of different Pakistani dishes that are considered to be curries. Lamb korma, chicken handi (HAHN-dee), and chicken karahi (kah-RAH-hee) are among the most popular.

Lamb korma is a type of dry curry. It is made with cubes of lamb cooked in yogurt sauce with sweet onions, juicy tomatoes, and hot and sweet spices such as cardamom, cinnamon, chili powder, and garam masala. Adding cinnamon to savory dishes is a cooking technique that came from the Persians—the ancient people of Iran—while using yogurt to make sauces may have

A man prepares a meal on a karahi, a round concave steel pot used by Pakistani cooks.

started in Afghanistan or India.

Chicken handi is a dish in which chicken is cooked in a spicy cream sauce. It is similar to foods prepared in India and Afghanistan. The dish gets its name from the pot it is cooked in, which is called a **handi**. It has a round, wide bottom and a narrow neck that holds in steam. It works much like a pressure cooker, which is a pot that cooks food at high temperatures and in less time than many other types of pots. It is unclear whether the handi was first used in India or Afghanistan, because cooking foods slowly is a tradition in both countries.

Chicken karahi is also made in a special pot. It is a rounded steel pot that is similar to a Chinese wok or frying pan. The way the dish is cooked also has Chinese roots. Unlike most curries, chicken karahi is stir-fried. Stir-frying is a Chinese cooking method that involves

Raita

Raita can be made in a variety of ways. Depending on the cook's taste, raita may contain cucumber, tomatoes, pineapple, chili peppers, different spices, mint, and/or cilantro. For thinner raita add a little water. It makes a good dip for kebabs or vegetables.

Ingredients
1 cup plain yogurt
½ cucumber, peeled and chopped
1 small tomato chopped
½ teaspoon garlic powder
¼ teaspoon ground cumin
1 teaspoon cilantro, chopped

Instructions
1. Mix all the ingredients together in a bowl.
2. Chill one hour before serving.
3. Serve cold.

Makes 1 cup.
Serves 4.

Raita is a yogurt-based dip eaten with kebabs or vegetables.

cooking food quickly over high heat while stirring.

To make chicken karahi, Pakistani cooks toss bite-sized morsels of chicken, chili peppers, tomatoes, garlic, and ginger into lots of sizzling oil. The cook shakes the pot back and forth while stirring the ingredients. In a few minutes, the chicken is coated with sauce and the dish is done. "The karahi dish is quick," explains Huma Qureshi. "The flavor comes from fresh chillis and chilli flakes that give it a hot kick that catches your throat in a satisfying way."[8]

Biryani

Curries are not the only foods that are often served with rice. Rice has been grown in Pakistan since about 2000 B.C. It has always been an important part of the Pakistani people's diet. Biryani (bee-ree-AH-nee) is a very popular dish that features alternating layers of rice and spiced meat. Historians believe the dish was first made in Persia (modern Iran). It may have been brought to Pakistan by the Moghuls. The Moghuls were central Asians who ruled what is now India and Pakistan from the 16th century until 1858.

Biryani is popular throughout south Asia and there are many varieties. Biryani can contain chicken, lamb, or vegetables. What is different about Pakistani biryani compared to biryani made in other nations is that Pakistan's version contains potatoes.

Making the dish is time consuming. To make it Pakistani cooks first fry whole spices, chili peppers, onions, and potatoes in oil. Next they add meat, veg-

Biryani, a popular dish with layers of meat and rice, is enjoyed throughout South Asia. Pakistani cooks make their version unique by adding potatoes.

etables, yogurt, and water and slowly cook the mixture until the meat is tender. The cook prepares the rice in a separate pot with spices and fried onions. When the rice is light and fluffy, the cook layers the rice and meat in a pan and puts it in the oven to bake. The whole process can take hours, but the delicious dish is well worth the effort. Of Pakistani biryani, a food photographer and blogger known as Fine China Girl says, "My dear Pakistani friend brought me chicken biryani that his mother made. He told me that his mother and sister spend at least four hours prepping and cooking it. . . . My words cannot do justice to this dish. . . [in which] you can taste the fusion [blending] of many flavors. . . . It's like there is a party in my mouth."[9]

Kebabs

Kebabs (kuh-BOBS) are another favorite Pakistani food. They originated in the Middle East and were brought to Pakistan by Arab invaders spreading the Islamic religion. Although most North Americans think of kebabs as grilled meat threaded through sticks called skewers and cooked over a charcoal fire, in Pakistan kebabs refer to any grilled meat. Skewered kebabs, however, are quite popular.

Pakistanis make many varieties of kebabs. Beef,

Pakistani Family Life

Most Pakistanis live in large extended family groups that include parents, children, grandparents, aunts, uncles, and cousins. They either all live in the same house or in houses that are grouped together. The oldest male relative in the extended family is considered to be the head of the family. He makes decisions involving the family and its members.

Elderly relatives are treated with great respect. Grandfathers have the honor of naming the babies. All elderly people are served food first, and they are given the best food. No one eats until the eldest family member starts to eat.

Most Pakistani women are mothers and homemakers, although some work outside the home. It is common for mothers to have many children. Not all children go to school. Girls, especially, may not go to school. Instead their mothers teach them how to become good homemakers.

Chicken tikka kebabs are one of several types of flavorful grilled meat dishes that are popular in Pakistan.

lamb, chicken, or ground meat are all made into kebabs. Shami (SHAH-mee) kebabs are made with ground beef. To make them cooks combine ground beef with ground garbanzo beans and spices. They form the mixture into little patties that look like miniature hamburgers but taste hotter and more unusual.

Tikka (TEE-kah) kebabs are other favorites. They are made of cubes of beef, chicken, or lamb that are **marinated** in a tart and zesty mixture of yogurt, lemon juice, and spices. This mixture flavors the meat and makes it melt-in-the-mouth tender. Bihari (bee-HAH-ree) kebabs are skewered chunks of beef rolled in spices. They are also popular.

No matter the type of kebab, the meat is always cooked until it is brown on the outside and juicy within. Kebabs are served with raita for dipping and hot roti or naan, which diners wrap around the meat.

Beef Tikka

Beef tikka can be grilled on or off a skewer. It can be cooked on a grill or in a broiler.

Ingredients
1 pound beef, cut into cubes
¼ cup plain yogurt
2 tablespoons lime juice
1 tablespoon olive oil
1 teaspoon minced garlic
½ teaspoon chili powder
½ teaspoon ginger

Instructions
1. Mix the yogurt, oil, lemon juice, and spices together. Put the meat in a bowl. Spoon the yogurt mixture over the meat and marinate in the refrigerator for 4 to 5 hours.
2. Heat a grill. Put the meat on skewers. Let the meat brown on one side, then turn the skewer. The meat is done when it is no longer pink inside.
3. Remove the meat from the skewers before serving.
4. Serve with raita or chutney.
Serves 4.

As a rule, Pakistani kebabs and other favorite dishes like biryani and curries are extremely flavorful. They reflect the country's rich history and culture as well as the talent and creativity of Pakistani cooks. Halai explains: "The diversity . . . of our culture is so rich, we have inherited all the . . . [different] food and are now getting to enjoy it all."[10]

Tea and Treats

Pakistanis like to snack. Pakistani markets and streets are full of snack stalls that prepare treats that taste great with a steaming cup of chai (cheye), or tea. Chai is the Pakistani people's favorite drink.

A Symbol of Hospitality and Friendship

There are tea shops and stalls all over Pakistan. Pakistanis drink chai all day long. In fact, tea is more than just a drink. Whether drunk alone or with a savory or sweet treat, tea is a big part of Pakistani life. Tea is served with breakfast. It is enjoyed with treats in the morning and afternoon, when almost everyone takes a tea break. Shopkeepers offer it to customers, and business meetings begin with tea. "There's this thing with

Two men sip tea from small cups at a tea shop in Pakistan. Tea drinking is a relatively new but very popular custom among the Pakistani people.

the people of Pakistan," says Don Sambandaraksa, a Thai reporter describing his experience in Pakistan. "Whatever the problem, whatever the situation, first they must offer you a cup of tea."[11]

Guests cannot leave a Pakistani home without drinking tea. In Pakistan sharing a cup of tea is a symbol of hospitality and friendship. A Pakistani proverb explains: "The first time you share tea . . . you are a stranger. The second time you take tea, you are an honored guest. The third time you share a cup of tea, you become family."[12]

Refreshing Snacks

Pakistani summers can be extremely hot, so cool drinks are especially satisfying in the summer months. Street vendors sell freshly squeezed juices that often contain a pinch of salt, which Pakistanis say is very refreshing in the heat. Carrot, apple, and pomegranate juices are quite popular. Mango lassi, a drink similar to a smoothie, is also very popular. It is made with chunks of sweet, ripe mango, milk, sugar, and yogurt.

Fresh fruit is also eaten. Mangoes, peaches, watermelon, grapes, pears, and oranges are all warm-weather favorites. So is ice cream. It is sold in ice cream parlors, or shops, and by street vendors pushing carts or riding tricycles. The vendors announce their arrival by blaring taped music. Each ice cream brand has its own musical jingle. Most vendors offer mango, chocolate, strawberry, pineapple, orange, and apple ice cream bars.

Mango lassi, a cool yogurt-based drink, is popular among Pakistanis, especially during the hot summer months.

Despite its popularity, tea drinking is a rather new custom in Pakistan. Although tea is grown in Asia, very little is grown in Pakistan. In the past, tea was not readily available and was not part of the Pakistani people's diet. Pakistanis did not drink tea until about 1900. At that time, the British owned almost all the tea plantations in India and they sold most of the tea to Europe. In an effort to expand their market to Pakistan, the British set up stalls on Pakistani streets offering passers-by a free cup of tea. It was love at first sip. According to Owais Mughal, the managing editor of the Pakistani cultural website called *All Things Pakistan,* "Tea drinking . . . is now our national habit, addiction, and part of our . . . culture."[13] In fact, Pakistan is now the third largest importer of tea in the world. Pakistan spends about $220 million a year buying tea from other countries.

Spiced, Pink, or Buttered

Pakistanis drink both green and black tea. They usually brew their tea with fragrant spices and add milk and sugar. To make tea Pakistanis add tea bags to boiling water in a pot. There should be one tea bag or teaspoon of tea per person, plus one for the pot. The mixture is left to **simmer**. Next are added the milk and a spice called cardamom. The crushed cardamom pods perfume the tea and give it a warm gingery flavor. Cinnamon, cloves, and nutmeg also may be added. When the flavors have blended, the tea is poured into a pretty teapot. The teapot is wrapped in a tea cozy, which is a decorative cloth that keeps the teapot warm. Then it is placed on a gleaming tray with dainty little teacups. Sugar is added to each teacup, and the tea is poured through a strainer into each cup. Author Huma Siddiqui explains: "Tea is served with a lot of pride and

A Pakistani woman presents a tray of tea prepared for guests at her home. Hosts in Pakistan serve tea as a sign of hospitality to their visitors.

great emphasis [importance] is placed on the way it is served; in a nice tea set accompanied with a tray and a beautiful tea cozy."[14]

Pink tea is also popular. Pink tea originated in Kashmir, a territory northwest of Pakistan that is partly ruled by Pakistan. Pink tea is a popular winter drink that, despite its name, is actually made from strong green tea. It is made in the same manner as regular tea except that baking soda is added to the pot while the tea is simmering. Substances in the baking soda neutralize acids in the tea and turn the liquid pink. Instead of sugar, cardamom and salt are added to the hot liquid. Before serving, the tea is topped with ground almonds and pistachio nuts. The nuts thicken the tea and add an earthy flavor and a nutty fragrance.

Butter tea is made in the same way as pink tea except a pat of yak's butter is added to the tea. Yaks are animals that are similar to buffalo. They are native to the Himalayan Mountains of northern Pakistan, where they are raised for milk. Butter tea originated in the Tibetan region of southwest China. Both butter tea and pink tea are rich and warming. Pakistanis say that these teas are especially soothing on chilly days.

Spiced Tea

This tea is delicious hot. It can also be chilled and served as iced tea.

Ingredients
4 cups water
5 tea bags, black tea
1 cinnamon stick
¼ teaspoon ground cardamom
pinch ground cloves
4 teaspoons sugar
4 tablespoons milk

Instructions
1. Boil the water and spices.
2. Transfer the water with spices into a teapot. Add the tea bags. Cover the teapot and let the tea bags steep, or soak in the liquid. (The longer they steep, the stronger the tea.)
3. Put a tablespoon of milk in each teacup. Pour in the tea, using a strainer. Add a teaspoon of sugar to each cup. Stir the mixture.

Serves 4.

Fried Treats

Delicious savory treats often are served with tea. Samosas, pakoras, and paras are favorite choices. All three are deep-fried. Deep-frying is a cooking method in which food is placed into hot oil and cooked until it is crisp on the outside and soft and moist on the inside.

Samosas are small triangular pastries that are stuffed with finely chopped lamb or boiled potatoes. The lamb or potatoes are mixed with chili peppers, green onions, and spices. Black onion seeds are often added to the dough to give the pastry a peppery flavor. The assortment of flavors is amazing. Samosas are sold on the streets of Pakistan. They are eaten throughout south and central Asia, northern Africa, and the Middle East. Historians think they originated in ancient Persia, and that Persian spice traders, who ate the small pastries as they traveled,

Samosas, deep-fried pastries stuffed with meat or potatoes and spices, are popular treats in Pakistan and throughout surrounding regions in Asia, Africa, and the Middle East.

A Diverse Place

Pakistan has many landforms, including beaches, deserts, plains, forests, hills, river valleys, and mountains. The Himalayas in northern Pakistan are some of the highest and most rugged mountains in the world. K2 is the second tallest peak in the world. It is located on the border between Pakistan and China. It measures 28,253 feet (8,612m) in height. It is nicknamed the "Savage Mountain." It can only be climbed in the summer because the weather is too cold and severe the rest of the year. Climbing K2 is so dangerous that climbers have a 27 percent chance of dying on the climb.

Pakistan's Indus River Valley is more forgiving. All of Pakistan's major rivers flow into the Indus River. It is one of the world's largest rivers. It flows from Tibet, through Pakistan, and to Bangladesh. Land around the river is fertile. Almost all the food grown in Pakistan is grown in the Indus River Valley.

brought samosas to Pakistan.

Pakoras are another favorite. They consist of tiny slices of potatoes, onions, or other vegetables that are mixed in a spicy batter made of ground garbanzo beans, chili powder, and water. The vegetables are deep-fried until they are hot and golden. The deep-fried snacks called paras do not contain a filling. These little crackers are simply crunchy, diamond-shaped bits of dough flavored with black onion seeds.

All three treats are eaten fresh and hot. They are often dipped in **chutney**, a sweet and spicy south

Asian relish similar to salsa. There are many varieties of chutney. Most are made up of small chunks of fruit and/or herbs mixed with spices. They are brightly colored and have a slightly sweet, slightly tart flavor. Tamarind chutney is especially popular. It is made with tamarind paste, cumin, chili powder, sugar, and water. Tamarinds are tart fruits that taste similar to sour prunes. Other favorite varieties of chutney feature tomatoes, green mangoes, mint, and coriander. Dipping hot fried treats in chutney helps cool them down and adds an interesting mix of flavors. "You gotta try it," insists Pakistani scientist Bilal Zuberi. "Deep fried spinach pakoras dipped in . . . imli (tamarind) chutni is unbelieveable."[15]

Sweet Snacks

Pakistanis also enjoy sweet treats with tea. Paras, for example, can be made with sugar instead of black-pepper seeds. Biscuits, the name Pakistanis give to cookies, are very popular. They may be homemade, freshly made in bakeries, or packaged in boxes. Some packaged biscuits such as chocolate chip and chocolate sandwich biscuits are much like the cookies sold in North American stores. Other biscuits are less familiar to North Americans. Many feature pistachio nuts. Naan khatai (nan ka-TIE) is a traditional favorite. It is a crunchy, crumbly cookie that is flavored with cardamom, and topped with ground pistachio nuts. Many Pakistani cooks make the cookies with **ghee**. It is butter in which all the milk solids have been removed. It is made by

Naan Khatai

These cookies are light and not too sweet. They are delicious with tea and are fairly simple to make.

Ingredients
1 cup flour
½ cup sugar
¼ teaspoon ground cardamom
1 tablespoon ground pistachio nuts
½ cup vegetable oil

Instructions
1. Preheat the oven to 375°F.
2. Combine the flour, cardamom, and sugar. Slowly add the oil. Add only enough oil so that the dough sticks together and can be formed into a ball.
3. Form the dough into 10 balls. Press the balls lightly between your hands so that they are about ¾-inch thick. Sprinkle each cookie with ground pistachio nuts.
4. Spray a cookie sheet with nonstick spray. Put the cookies on the sheet about 1 inch apart. Bake until the cookies are golden brown, about 15 minutes.

Makes 10 cookies.

Naan khatai cookies are often served with tea in Pakistan.

Ghee, a form of butter from which the milk solids have been removed, is frequently used by Pakistanis as an ingredient in cookies and other dishes.

slowly heating unsalted butter until all the moisture cooks out. Pakistani cooks often use it in place of butter or oil. Ghee is fragrant. Combining it with cardamom makes a delightfully scented cookie. According to a Pakistani cook named Ambus, the cookie is "extremely light but sweet and just melts in your mouth."[16]

Sharing a pot of tea accompanied by naan khatai or other sweet or savory treats is a delicious part of Pakistani life. It represents hospitality and friendship to Pakistanis and is considered a very satisfying snack.

Chapter 4

Celebrating with Food

Pakistanis like to get together with family and friends, share food, and celebrate. Special occasions and holidays are a perfect time to do this. Traditional foods are a part of every celebration.

Fasting and Feasting

Pakistan is a nation mainly made up of Muslims. Muslims are believers in the Islamic faith. Most Pakistani holidays are tied to Islamic religious holy days. **Ramadan** (RAHM-ah-dahn) is especially important. This month-long holiday usually falls in the late summer or early autumn. For an entire month, Muslims typically fast during daylight hours in an effort to cleanse their souls. Fasting involves giving up all food and drink.

A Pakistani man prepares plates of food to serve for iftar, the evening meal that breaks the daily fast that Muslims observe during Ramadan.

Daily meals are limited to two suhoor, (SOO-hoor), a predawn meal that starts the daily fast, and **iftar,** the evening meal that breaks it.

After a day of fasting, Pakistanis look forward to iftar. Much planning usually goes into the menu, and the guest list is typically large. Sharing the iftar meal with others is an important part of the holiday. In fact, no one is supposed to eat iftar alone. Families gather at the house of the most senior family member each night for the meal. Friends, neighbors, and even strangers are welcomed, too.

Iftar Foods

Traditionally, the iftar meal begins with dates. Dates are sweet fruits similar to figs. The Muslim prophet Muhammad began the custom of breaking the daily fast with dates in the 7th century. Dates are nutritious, light, and easy to digest, which makes them a good food to eat on an empty stomach. Pakistanis eat both fresh and dried dates. They often remove the seeds

Popular Sports

Pakistanis enjoy eating samosas and spiced nuts as they watch their favorite sports. Cricket is the most popular sport in Pakistan. It is a team sport that is played with two paddle-shaped bats, hard balls, and two wickets, which are located at both ends of the playing field. The wickets consist of two wooden crosspieces that rest on three wooden stumps. The object of the game is to score runs by hitting the ball and running between the wickets. Pakistan's national cricket team won the Cricket World Cup in 1992 and was a runner-up in 1999.

Field hockey is also very popular. It is a form of hockey that is played with a ball on a grassy field. Players do not wear skates. Pakistani field hockey teams have won three Olympic gold medals. Polo is another major sport. Polo is played on horseback with players hitting a ball into their opponent's goal while swinging a mallet. In Pakistan, polo is generally played by teams from the Pakistani army. Pakistani's national polo team ranks among the top teams in the world.

A man sells dates at a market in Pakistan. Dates are sweet fruits that are customarily eaten to begin iftar, the evening meal served during Ramadan.

and fill the fruit with ground pistachio nuts or ground almonds. Dates are also rolled in coconut flakes or are covered with warq (wahrk). Warq is a shiny, edible foil that makes each date look like a little jewel.

A refreshing, cool drink is always served with the dates. Rooh Afza (roo AHF-zah) is a red syrup that comes bottled like soda. It is an especially popular choice. The syrup is made of sugar, citrus and vegetable juices, orange and lemon blossoms, cooling herbs, and rosewater. Rosewater is a fragrant liquid made with rose petals and water. It gives Rooh Afza a delicate floral scent. The syrup is concentrated and must be diluted with water or milk before drinking. Even when diluted, Rooh Afza is extremely sweet.

Rooh Afza is very energizing. In fact, it was created in 1907 as a health remedy made to enliven and strengthen people. Like many modern sports drinks, Rooh Afza contains substances that help replace minerals that the body loses from sweating. It is an especially good drink for thirsty Pakistanis who have abstained from drinking any liquids for eight to ten hours. For this reason it almost always is drunk at the start of the iftar meal. Adil Najam, the founding editor of the *All Things Pakistan* website, explains: "One of the many things that is a near necessary feature of the Pakistani Iftar spread is Rooh Afza. . . .The unstated rule seems [to be] that there cannot be Ramzan [Ramadan], or at least Iftar, in Pakistan without Rooh Afza."[17]

Fruit Salad

The rest of the iftar menu varies. Popular choices include samosas, curries, kebabs, and channa chaat, which is made with garbanzo beans cooked with tomatoes, pota-

toes, and spices. Fruit chat, a spicy fruit salad, is almost always on the menu, too. It contains a mixture of fresh, juicy fruits such as mangoes, apples, banana, pineapple, apricots, and grapes. The fruit is cut into small cubes and sprinkled with salt, pepper, sugar, lemon juice, and chaat masala. The juice in the fruit helps quench diners' thirst and provides them with valuable nutrients. Some cooks add fresh vegetables like carrots and sweet onions to the salad. Others add cream, giving the salad a rich taste and texture. But with or without cream,

A Pakistani man offers bananas, mangoes, and other fruits for sale at an outdoor market. A mix of fresh fruit is used to make fruit chaat, a spicy salad sometimes served for iftar.

Celebrating with Food

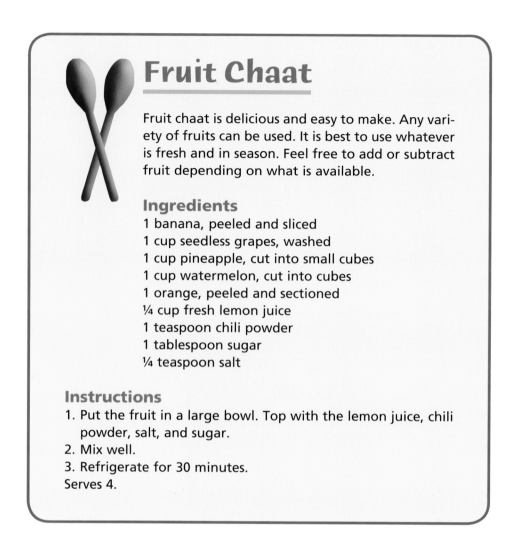

Fruit Chaat

Fruit chaat is delicious and easy to make. Any variety of fruits can be used. It is best to use whatever is fresh and in season. Feel free to add or subtract fruit depending on what is available.

Ingredients

1 banana, peeled and sliced
1 cup seedless grapes, washed
1 cup pineapple, cut into small cubes
1 cup watermelon, cut into cubes
1 orange, peeled and sectioned
¼ cup fresh lemon juice
1 teaspoon chili powder
1 tablespoon sugar
¼ teaspoon salt

Instructions

1. Put the fruit in a large bowl. Top with the lemon juice, chili powder, salt, and sugar.
2. Mix well.
3. Refrigerate for 30 minutes.

Serves 4.

fruit chaat is very tasty. It mixes different flavors, tasting sweet, tart, salty, and zesty all at the same time.

Sweet Noodles

When Ramadan ends, Pakistanis mark the end of fasting with a joyous festival known as Eid ul-Fitr Fitr (ide uhl-FET-ter). During this three-day holiday, Pakistanis exchange gifts, children get new clothes, money is donated to the poor, families and friends visit each other, and a special food called seviyan (seh-VEE-ahn) is served. It is a sweet noodle dish that symbolizes the sweetness and joy of Eid ul-Fitr. It is made with vermicelli (ver-muh-CHELL-ee) noodles, which are small, thin noodles similar to angel-hair pasta. To make seviyan, cooks first brown the noodles in butter. Then they cook the noodles in milk flavored with sugar and cardamom. Some cooks use khoya instead of milk. Khoya is milk in which most of the moisture has been removed. It is similar to condensed milk. Seviyan made with khoya is thick like pudding, while seviyan made with milk is more like porridge.

When the noodles are soft, the seviyan is ready. It is eaten hot, topped with raisins, crushed pistachio nuts, and/or almonds. It has a mouthwatering aroma and a creamy taste. Seviyan is often eaten for breakfast during Eid ul-Fitr, and it is customarily served to visitors along with tea and other sweets. According to Pakistani chef Zakir Qureshi, "[Seviyan] is considered an essential dish which is prepared and served to guests on Eid-ul-Fitr as a sweet dish. People like it very much."[18]

Wedding Treats

Sweets also play a big role in Pakistani weddings, which are typically huge celebrations that last for three days. It is not unusual for hundreds of guests to be invited to the festivities in which mountains of food are served. In fact, Pakistani weddings are often so grand that parents start saving for the wedding when a child is born.

Seviyan

Seviyan is not difficult to make. Vermicelli noodles are sold in the pasta section of supermarkets.

Ingredients
1 cup vermicelli noodles, broken into small pieces
1 tablespoon butter
1 cup sweetened condensed milk
2 cups milk
1 tablespoon each raisins, chopped almonds, chopped pistachio nuts
1 teaspoon ground cardamom

Instructions
1. Melt the butter in a frying pan on medium heat. Add the vermicelli noodles. Fry until the noodles are lightly browned.
2. Put the milk in another pot. Bring it to a boil. Add the condensed milk, raisins, cardamom, vermicelli, and nuts. Cook uncovered on medium-low heat until the mixture thickens and the vermicelli is soft.

Serve hot. Serves 4.

Seviyan is a sweet treat usually topped with raisins and pistachios.

National Parks

Pakistan has many national parks that were established to protect native plants and wildlife. Farming, mining, and hunting are not permitted in the parks, but visitors are welcome. Some parks allow camping and have museums. Scientists conduct research in some of the parks. Because animals are protected in the parks, those species of animals that were near extinction, or about to die out, are now making a comeback. These include snow leopards, Himalayan brown bears, and Marco Polo sheep. These sheep are about twice the size of other wild or farm-raised sheep. The males have large spiral-shaped curving horns that hunters used to take as trophies.

Other animals that make their home in the national parks include more than 100 species of birds such as vultures, golden eagles, and pheasants, snakes like cobras and pit vipers, crocodiles, turtles, rhinos, gazelles, different varieties of wild goats, leopards and other wild cats, wolves, foxes, and macaque monkeys.

The festivities begin the day before the wedding with the mehndi (MEN-dee) party. *Mehndi* is the Urdu word for henna, a red vegetable dye that is used in Pakistan to create temporary tattoos. Usually, there are two separate mehndi parties, one for the bride and another for the groom. At the bride's party, the female guests draw complicated designs on the bride's feet and hands with henna. Often the groom's name is drawn into the designs. At both parties, the bride and groom

A fresh batch of gulab jamun, a pastry traditionally served to Pakistani brides and grooms before their weddings, is covered in sweet syrup.

are fed a sweet treat known as gulab jamun (GOO-lahb JAH-muhn), so that they will have a happy married life. Gulab jamun is a small, round fried pastry ball covered with fragrant warm syrup made from rosewater, sugar and cardamom, and topped with sliced almonds. The bride and groom are encouraged to eat lots of the sticky treat. The more they eat, the sweeter their married life is supposed to be.

The next day the couple is married. Once the ceremony is over, a multicourse feast is served. The high point of the feast is the dessert table, which is loaded with delicious sweets. Bread pudding, rice pudding, and halwa, a rich, thick pudding made with carrots mixed with dried fruit and nuts, are all part of the spread. Kheer, or rice pudding, is so important that before the bride and groom leave the reception the groom feeds the bride the pudding out of his hands. Since most Pakistani marriages are arranged by the couple's parents and the bride and groom usually do not know each other well before marrying, this tradition is supposed to draw the couple closer together.

The festivities do not end until the next day, when the groom's family hosts a big dinner party in which foods like biryani and lamb korma are served. The guests leave with full stomachs and happy memories. Indeed, the traditional foods served during holidays and special occasions help make Pakistani celebrations all the more fun and memorable.

Metric Conversions

Mass (weight)

1 ounce (oz.)	= 28.0 grams (g)
8 ounces	= 227.0 grams
1 pound (lb.) or 16 ounces	= 0.45 kilograms (kg)
2.2 pounds	= 1.0 kilogram

Liquid Volume

1 teaspoon (tsp.)	= 5.0 milliliters (ml)
1 tablespoon (tbsp.)	= 15.0 milliliters
1 fluid ounce (oz.)	= 30.0 milliliters
1 cup (c.)	= 240 milliliters
1 pint (pt.)	= 480 milliliters
1 quart (qt.)	= 0.96 liters (l)
1 gallon (gal.)	= 3.84 liters

Pan Sizes

8-inch cake pan	= 20 x 4-centimeter cake pan
9-inch cake pan	= 23 x 3.5-centimeter cake pan
11 x 7-inch baking pan	= 28 x 18-centimeter baking pan
13 x 9-inch baking pan	= 32.5 x 23-centimeter baking pan
9 x 5-inch loaf pan	= 23 x 13-centimeter loaf pan
2-quart casserole	= 2-liter casserole

Temperature

212°F	= 100°C (boiling point of water)
225°F	= 110°C
250°F	= 120°C
275°F	= 135°C
300°F	= 150°C
325°F	= 160°C
350°F	= 180°C
375°F	= 190°C
400°F	= 200°C

Length

¼ inch (in.)	= 0.6 centimeters (cm)
½ inch	= 1.25 centimeters
1 inch	= 2.5 centimeters

Notes

Chapter 1: An Artful Blend

1. "Pakistani Cooking, as Spicy as It Gets." KhanaPakana.com.www .khanapakana.com/pakistani-recipes/pakistani-recipes.html.

2. Humma Siddiqui. *Jasmine in Her Hair*. Madison, WI: White Jasmine, 2003, p. 27.

3. Shayma. "Dal (Lentils) in the Pakistani/Afghan Manner." The Spice Spoon, March 21, 2010. www.thespicespoon.com/blog /lentils/.

4. Imaan. "Dadi's Village Part Two." Imaan.net. http://imaan.net /category/food-glorious-food/.

5. Halai. "Please Sir May I Have Some More—Oliver Twist." The Rain on Your Parade, July 16, 2009. http://abbasbytwo.wordpress .com/2009/07/16/please-sir-may-i-have-some-more-oliver-twist/.

Chapter 2: A Mix of Cultures

6. Jennifer Brennan. *The Cuisines of Asia*. New York: St. Martin's, 1984, p. 326.

7. Huma Qureshi. "Pakistani Food: Cooking from the Heart." *Times* (London), June 3, 2010. www.timesonline.co.uk/tol/life_and_ style/food_and_drink/article7142628.ece.

8. Huma Qureshi. "Pakistani Food: Cooking from the Heart."

9. "Homemade Chicken Biryani—Pakistani Style." finechinagirl, July 4, 2009. http://finechinagirl.com/2009/07/04/homemade-chicken-biryani-pakistani-style/.

10. Halai. "Please Sir May I Have Some More—Oliver Twist.

Chapter 3: Tea and Treats

11. Quoted in Aamir Attaa. "Getting a Pakistani SIM for Foreigners Isn't Dalawa." Pro Pakistani, June 23, 2010. http://propakistani .pk/2010/06/23/pakistani-sim-for-foreigners/.

12. Sam Jones. "Greg Mortenson: The U.S. Army's Local Guide to Afghanistan and Pakistan." *The Guardian,* July 19, 2010. www .guardian.co.uk/world/2010/jul/19/greg-mortenson-us-army-afghanistan-pakistan.

13. Owais Mughal. "How Much Tea Does Pakistan Drink?" *All Things Pakistan,* June 3, 2007. http://pakistaniat.com/2007/06/03 /pakistan-tea-consumption-chai-house-import-economy/.

14. Huma Siddiqui. "Tea Time." White Jasmine. http://whitejasmine .com/more_about/tea.html.

15. Bilel Zuberi. "Recipe of the Day—Pakora—Most Favorite Food During Ramadan." BZ Notes, October 10, 2006. http://bznotes .wordpress.com/2006/10/10/recipeof-the-day-pakora-most-favorite-food-during-ramadan/.

16. Ambus. "Naan Khatai or Sugar Cookies." Group Recipes. www .grouprecipes.com/30987/naan-khatai-or-sugar-cookies.html.

Chapter 4: Celebrating with Food

17. Adil Najam. "Ramzan, Rooh Afza, and Pakistani 'Red Bull.'" *All Things Pakistan,* September 30, 2008. http://pakistaniat .com/2008/09/30/rooh-afza-milk-red-bull-pakistan/.

18. Quoted in "Khoya Seviyan Vermicelli." KhanaPakana. com. www.khanapakana.com/recipe/templates/cooking-recipe.aspx?articleid=626B4EC6-6DBC-4726-A8D6-46F827B90789&zoneid=348.

Glossary

chutney: A sweet and spicy relish.

curry: Any dish in which meat, chicken, fish, or vegetables are cooked in a spicy sauce.

dal: A creamy stew-like dish made with mashed legumes.

ghee: Butter in which all the milk solids have been removed.

handi: A pot with a round, wide bottom and a narrow neck that holds in steam.

iftar: The nightly meal that breaks the Ramadan daily fast.

Islam: The name of the religion Muslims follow. It is based on the teachings of the prophet Muhammad and the holy book, the Koran.

legumes: Plants such as beans, lentils, and peas.

marinated: To have soaked food in liquid before cooking in order to add flavor.

masala: A blend of ground spices used in Pakistani cooking

Moghuls: Central Asian people who ruled Pakistan for over 200 years.

mortar: A small stone dish in which spices are ground.

naan: Flat, round yeast bread.

pestle: A small club-like tool used to grind spices into a powder.

Ramadan: A month-long holiday in which Muslims typically fast during daylight hours in an effort to purify their souls

roti: Round flat bread made without yeast.

simmer: To cook food gently at a temperature below the boiling point.

tandoor: A beehive shape clay oven that cooks at high temperatures.

tarka: Spiced oil used to flavor Pakistani cooking.

tawa: A flat iron griddle in which roti is often baked.

Urdu: Pakistan's national language.

For Further Exploration

Books

J. M. Bedell. *Teens in Pakistan.* Mankato, MN: Compass Point, 2009. Gives information about Pakistan by examining the daily lives of young Pakistanis.

Paul Harrison and Geoff Barker. *Pakistan.* London: Hodder Wayland, 2010. Information about Pakistan's geography, climate, people, family life, religion, and economics with maps and charts.

Andrew Langley. *Pakistan.* London: Franklin Watts, 2010. Discusses Pakistan's geography, government, and life of the people.

Sarah Thomson (adapter), Greg Mortenson, and David Oliver Relin. *Three Cups of Tea: A Man's Journey to Change the History of the World One Child at a Time.* New York: Puffin, 2009. This book, which is adapted for children, is the true story of an injured mountain climber who was saved by Pakistani villagers. In return he built schools in Pakistani villages. His experiences tell a lot about Pakistani culture and daily life.

Websites

Central Intelligence Agency, "The World Fact-book Pakistan" (www.cia.gov/library/publications/the-world-factbook/geos/pk.html). This website provides information on Pakistan's geography, economy, people, government, and current challenges. A map is included.

Food by Country, "Pakistan" (www.foodbycountry.com/Kazakhstan-to-South-Africa/Pakistan.html). This website discusses Pakistan's geography, foods and culture, and includes recipes.

Time for Kids, "Around the World Pakistan" (www.timeforkids.com/TFK/teachers/aw/wr/article/0,28138,1612040,00.html). Information about Pakistan including a timeline, fact file, words in Urdu, and a map with historical sites can be found on this colorful website.

Index

Picture Credits

About the Author

Barbara Sheen is the author of more than 60 books for young people. She lives in New Mexico with her family. In her spare time, she likes to swim, walk, garden, and read. Of course she loves to cook!